wah?

The Worst Book Ever

by

JAKE RONAN

There is a guy who wants to climb a BIG hill.

"Wha? Why?"

So, he started to climb the BIG hill.

"Purpose unknown, so far."

But, a tornado challenged him to a boxing match.

"Wha? Really?"

So, he KO'd it with one punch.

"He knocked out a tornado?"

Confused? You will be.

"That tornado had boxing gloves! wow."

K:0

Then, a bandit appeared, with a gun, and got hit in the face with a rock.

"Okay, a random bandit. Why not. Everything else seems crazy. Who threw the rock, by the way?"

So, with the bandit gone, the man went on climbing.

"For what purpose, we still don't know."

Finally... He reached the top.

"Yes, we'll get to see why now?"

Then he came back down.

"Wha? We don't get to find out why?"

And he went back to
his house.

"But why did he go up
the hill?"

But then his house blew up.

"Serves him right for not telling us why he went up the hill.

But, wha?

His house blew up? Why?"

So, he went to the bank to get a loan.

"Okay, now I feel sorry for him. He has to depend on a bank?!

P.S. Does he have insurance?"

And he bought a new house.

"Near a BIG hill so he can go climb it?"

So, he went to a pool
for a bit.

"To cool off after all that
activity, wha?"

Before he went home.

"Without any explanation of all these events?"

THE
END

The End

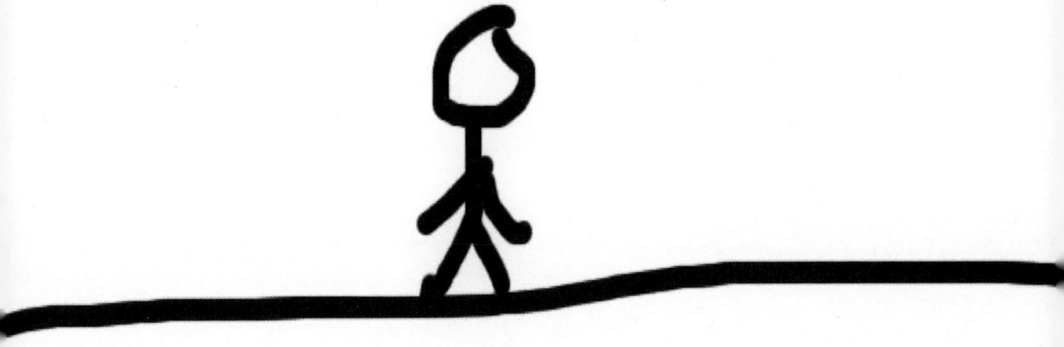

Printed in Great Britain
by Amazon

22071333R00018